What are the people saying to Jack? Why?

Let's read the title together: 'Be Quiet!'

Walkthrough

This is the back cover.

Let's read the blurb together.

Walkthrough

Look at the picture – these are the things Jack bought at the cinema. What are they?

Let's re-read the title: 'Be Quiet!'

Read the names of the author, the illustrator and the publisher.

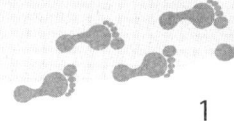

Walkthrough

Jack and his dad went to the cinema.
What did Dad get?
What do you think the film is about?
How can you tell?

Jack and his dad went to the cinema.
Dad got the tickets.

2

Observe and Prompt

If a child has difficulty reading 'went', prompt him/her to look at the initial letter and to think of a word that would make sense. Ask him/her to re-read the sentence.

Walkthrough

What did Jack get?

Jack got the popcorn and the drinks.

 Observe and Prompt

Check the children can read 'popcorn'; if not, prompt them to use picture and initial letter cues. If necessary, prompt them to break the word down into two small words.

Check children read 'drinks' paying attention to the plural.

Walkthrough

Where are Jack and his dad now?

Jack looks excited.

What do you think he says?

What do the people around him say?

What part of the film does Jack like best?

What sound would a rocket make?

The film began.
"I like this film," said Jack.
"I like the rockets. Whoosh!"

👁 Observe and Prompt

If a child has difficulty reading 'film', supply the word and ask him/her to re-read the sentence.

If a child has difficulty with 'whoosh', ask him/her to look at the 'wh' at the beginning of the word and the 'sh' at the end and think about what sound rockets make.

"Shhhh!" everyone said.

Walkthrough

What is Jack eating? Does he like popcorn?

What sound does popcorn make when you eat it? (*crunch*)

How do the people near to Jack feel?

Jack crunched his popcorn.
"I like this popcorn," he said.

6

Observe and Prompt

Observe one-to-one correspondence, checking that 'this' is not omitted.

If a child has difficulty reading 'this', ask him/her to look at the first two letters 'th' and to sound out the phoneme.

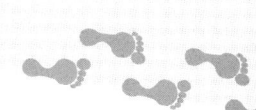

"Shhhh!" everyone said.

Walkthrough

What is Jack doing now?

Do you think he likes the drink?

What sound does he make when he is drinking? (*slurp*)

What does everyone else say?

Jack slurped his drink.
"I like this drink," he said.

Observe and Prompt

Check the children read with expression appropriate to the exclamation mark.

"Shhhh!" everyone said.

Walkthrough

What happened next?

Where do you think Jack is going?

Can you read the sign on the door?

What did everyone say? What are they feeling?

Jack got up. He wanted to go to the toilet.

👁 Observe and Prompt

If a child has difficulty reading 'wanted', ask him/her to notice 'ed' at the end of the word. Ask him/her to re-read the sentence so that it makes sense.

"Shhhh!" everyone said.

Walkthrough

Jack sees his friend. What does he say?

Can you find the boy's name in the text and read it? (*Ben*)

What happened next?

Then Jack saw a friend. "Hello Ben," he said.

Observe and Prompt

Check for appropriate expression and intonation when reading the dialogue.

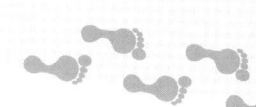

"**Be quiet!**" everyone said.

Walkthrough

What happened when the film was finished?

What did everyone do?

What has happened to Dad?

What does Jack say?

The film ended.
Everyone got up to go.

Observe and Prompt

If a child has difficulty reading 'Everyone', ask the child to turn back to page 13 to find a similar word. Point out the capital letter 'E' and then ask him/her to re-read the sentence.

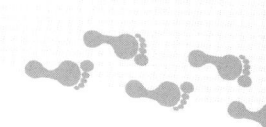

"Come on, Dad," said Jack, but Dad was asleep.

Walkthrough

What did Jack say to the people?

What do they think about Dad falling asleep?

How can you tell? What would you do if you were Jack?

"Shhhh everyone! My dad's asleep," said Jack.

Observe and Prompt

Check the children use an appropriate voice for 'My dad's asleep', e.g. in a whisper.